TRAVEL

Travel

25 Years Of Travel – 114 Countries

Andy Lee Graham

EverydayHobo.com HoboTraveler Inc.

CONTENTS

PARIS, FRANCE

KO PHA NGAN, THAILAND

TOGO, WEST AFRICA CHILDREN

MACHU PICCHU, TRAIN – CUSCO, PERU

LAOS, SOUTHEAST ASIA

BENIN, WEST AFRICA

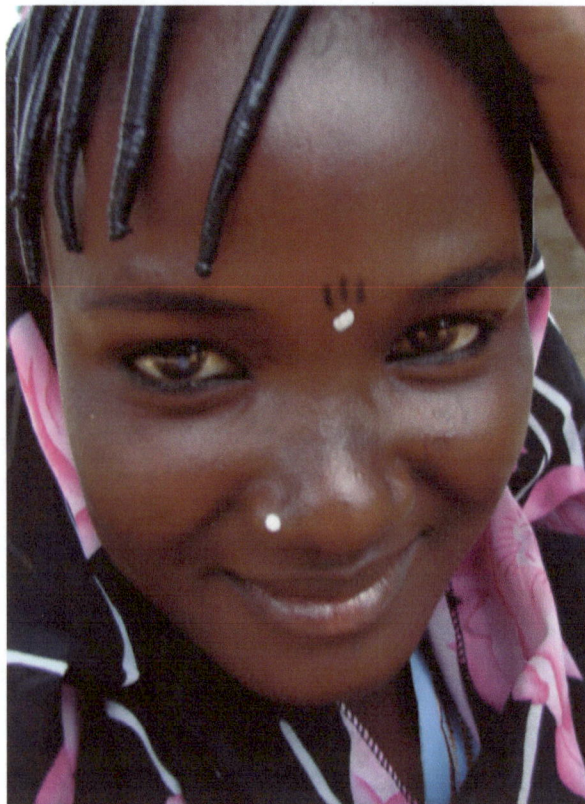

NEAR UNCONTACTED TRIBES – BREU, PERU

BABYLON, IRAQ

CHECKPOINT CHARLIE, BERLIN, GERMANY

SADHU HAMPI, INDIA

LAKE ATITLAN, GUATEMALA

YURT TENT, MONGOLIA

ANDY LEE GRAHAM AT BABYLON, IRAQ

THAILAND BEACH

RURRENABAQUE, BOLIVIA

DHAKA, BANGLADESH

KATHMANDU, NEPAL

TIBET

SEARCH FOR UNCONTACTED TRIBE

AFRICAN GIRL

KARA, TOGO WEST AFRICA

INDIA

PANAJACHEL, GUATEMALA

IVORY COAST

THAILAND MONKS

MASS GRAVE HILA, IRAQ

INDIA SCHOOL

CHASING RHINOS IN NEPAL

Who Andy Wants To Be

Everyday Hobo

Join $1

CASA ARGENTINA'S 8-37

Andy Lee Graham
Xela, Guatemala
Casa Argentina's
Hotel 1998-1999

EVERYDAYHOBO.COM
HOBOTRAVELER.COM

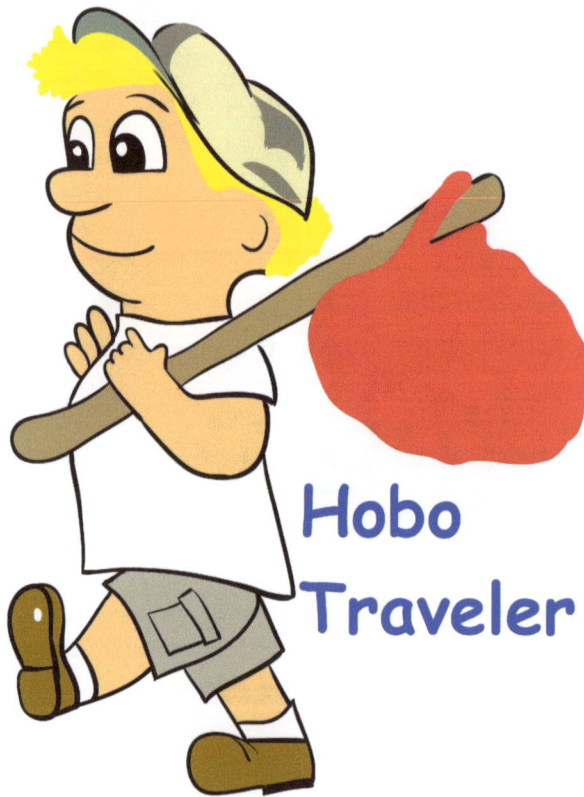

Hobo
Traveler

LIFE IS GOOD

Thank you for looking at my world; behind each photo is a story.

Today is June 10, 2023, I am writing this in the city of San Jose, Costa Rica, in room number 15 of the Costa Rica Backpackers Hostel.

Today, I will look at your photos on EverydayHobo.com, and remember, each photo is a story of your life.

Life is good.
Thank the good Gods.

Andy Lee Graham
hoboontheroad@yahoo.com

www.ingramcontent.com/pod-product-compliance
Lightning Source LLC
Chambersburg PA
CBHW041539260326
41914CB00015B/1504